RAMADAN NIGHTS

Adam was seven years old, and his little sister, **Hana**, was five. They really wanted to fast for **Ramadan**.

But **Mummy** and **Daddy** said,
"You are too small;
you can fast when you are much bigger."

Adam and **Hana** decided
to wake up for **Sehri**.

This is the early morning meal
before a **Ramadan** fast.

They hoped this would show
they were **big** enough
to be able to **fast.**

The next morning, **Adam** and **Hana**
woke up very early.

Everyone else in the house
was still **asleep!**

So, they went downstairs to wait
for the rest of the family to wake up.

Unfortunately they fell asleep and missed Sehri!

The next night they tried again.

Once again, they woke up
too early!

Everyone was still asleep!

Hana loved looking at **stars**.
That night, they seemed to **shine**
more **brightly** than ever before.

Adam loved the **silence**
at this time of night.
The **silence** felt like
it was full of **magic.**

Determined to stay awake, they decided to sit outside in the garden, looking over the town.

Together, they sat quietly enjoying the **beauty** of the **night sky.**

Adam remembered how their **Grandma** had told him that the **Prophet Muhammad**, peace and blessings upon him, loved praying at night.

"Shall we say a **prayer** together?" **Adam** asked **Hana**.

"What is a **prayer**?" asked **Hana**.

"A **prayer** is when we close our eyes
and imagine something beautiful
we want to happen and ask **Allah**,"
said **Adam**, remembering what their **Daddy**
had told him about **prayer**.

She prayed the world would be filled with happiness.

Adam closed his eyes and imagined everyone in the world being **friends** with each other.

When **Hana** opened her eyes,
she saw the most amazing thing.

"Look at the houses!"
she said to **Adam** with excitement.

"The **stars** are all the **prayers**, coming together, from every house," said **Grandma,** who had quietly arrived and stood behind them.

"This is the **magic** created from **Prayer** and **Meditation**," **Grandma** said.

Soon the **whole family** stood watching the magical **starry** night.

Beneath the **starry** night,
Adam and **Hana** fell asleep.

Perhaps they **were** too small to fast.

But they were **not** too small
to fall in love with **Ramadan,**
because they found
the **magic of the night prayer.**

Divine Breathings

The Prophet said, "In these days
the breathings of God prevail:
Keep ear and mind attentive
to these spiritual influences;
catch these breathings."

The Divine breathing came,
beheld you, and departed:
it gave life to whom it would, and left.
Another breathing has arrived.
Pay attention, friend,
don't miss this one, too.

~ Rumi

RAMADAN NIGHTS

Written and illustrated by uzma taj
First published in 2025

Text copyright © uzma taj 2025
Artwork copyright © uzma taj 2025
Digital Brushes by Lisa Glanz
"Divine Breathings" by Rumi from *The Rumi Daybook*, translated by Kabir & Camille Helminski, Shambhala Publications.

All rights reserved. No part of this publication may be reproduced, distributed, or transmitted in any form or by any means, including photocopying, recording, or other electronic or mechanical methods, without the author's prior written permission. For permission requests, see the website uzmataj.com. A reviewer may quote a brief passage in a review.

A CIP record for this book is available from the British Library.

Hardback ISBN: 9781739475796
Paperback ISBN: 9781739475741

uzmataj.com
Instagram @utaj

...and by the same author,
a magical tale with an Owl and a Boy
who wants to fly

A heart-warming tale of a young boy's
journey through nature, where he discovers the beauty
of the world around him and the joy of being himself.

About the author

uzma taj is an author and illustrator based in the scenic hills of Cumbria. She draws inspiration from nature's quiet magic and the spaces between moments. Often found wandering the countryside with a notebook in hand, uzma captures her ideas from the everyday wonder around her—wonder sparked by questions like, 'Am I both the star that shines and the one who dreams of meeting it?' Her art and storytelling invite readers to pause, imagine, and explore the beauty hidden in simple moments.

Building a world where every child feels safe to...

STRETCH

www.ingramcontent.com/pod-product-compliance
Lightning Source LLC
Chambersburg PA
CBRC092222090526
44583CB00009BA/188